Channelling the Inner Fire

Ignatian Spirituality in 15 Points

Brendan McManus SJ

ISBN: 9781788125314

Cover Image: istockphoto.com
Designed by Messenger Publications Design Department
Typeset in Adobe Garamond Pro, Bebas Neue and Storefront Pro
Printed by GPS Colour Graphics

Messenger Publications,
37 Leeson Place, Dublin D02 E5V0, Ireland
www.messenger.ie

Contents

Introduction

As a Jesuit priest my job is to help people find God in their lives, participate in building a better, fairer world, and lead more satisfying, fulfilling lives. As a priest, I meet a lot of good people, who I would describe as genuine 'searchers'. They often have great desires and a passion to build a better world but can't seem to direct or sustain that energy, often getting burnt out or disillusioned. I find people often lack the practical knowledge and tools needed to advance spiritually. The idea of faith they have inherited is not helpful. It imagines faith to be all or nothing, to be almost magical or miraculous in nature. This idea does not do justice to the complex nature of humanity and of contemporary life.

This booklet is an attempt to provide you with some of that practical knowledge. I look at my own experiences and those of Ignatius Loyola to articulate a different vision of the role faith and religious belief can play in your life. My approach is rooted in theology, but also comes out of my own life and vocational experience. Before I became a priest, I had a lucrative career in computer science. I became disillusioned with my career and eventually found happiness in my vocation as a priest. This booklet outlines the story of my discovery of the Jesuit or Ignatian method, which is based on the teachings of Ignatius Loyola, founder of the Jesuits. It is a practical and concrete method. It is based on experience and deals with the complexities of life. All of life's trials and triumphs are considered.

Ignatian Spirituality

Ignatian or Jesuit spirituality is a certain approach or method, different to Franciscan, Benedictine or Carmelite spirituality, that has a number of specific characteristics. It is based on internal experience (Ignatius was called the first psychologist) and is experiential, holistic (God is present in all of our life), practical, geared towards making decisions and taking actions; it is geared towards making a better world (justice) and taking up our role in that (vocation).

The 'faith problem'

Sometimes you can find no answer to your questions in Church and religious services or mass can seem dry, irrelevant and even empty. The Christianity you were brought up with seems inadequate to face the challenges and pressures of the modern world. There is a fire in your soul but you can't harness it in a constructive way. Despite being a genuine searcher, you can't find the answers you're looking for in today's Church. Does God not exist or are you looking in the wrong place?

What I call the 'faith problem' is the static image of God that informs the faith so many people have inherited from parents, the Church and wider society. It's not that this image of God is wrong, it's that it is 'one-dimensional'. It is what might be called a 'childhood' or even 'institutional' image of God, and it was passively received when growing up. Most people instinctively understand that human beings go through various stages of growth, where insights and wisdom are gained over time and in steps. The same is true of spiritual life. You have to develop a personalised faith that is in keeping with your own personal growth and development. Your 'childhood' image of God needs to be critiqued and reconstructed, so that it becomes more mature, integrated and personal.

Often this static or institutional image of God over-emphasises the miraculous or dramatic quality of religious belief, and all the while God is working away quietly but persistently within your life (a gentle breeze instead of a huge storm, cf. 1 Kings 19). Sometimes this inherited image of God is even negative or unhelpful. God is imagined as judge, patriarch, rule-maker, punisher, and so on. It is no wonder that you might find such a God unapproachable!

Talking from experience

From my own experience of re-finding faith in my late twenties, spirituality was a surprise to me. Rather than looking outside to rules, doctrines and teaching, I found something radically different. The miracle was that there was something going on *inside* me, within my very life experience. It was like an inner compass, GPS, or extra sense. It was there all the time, even though I hadn't noticed it, giving me messages and guidance on decisions.

I ignored it for such an incredibly long time, and it was only illness and reaching the end of my tether that eventually forced me to pay attention to this inner world. It is messy and volatile of course, this whole area of feelings, impulses and drives, but there is a certain truth to be found there. I found some of the most important answers there for my own journey. It seemed chaotic and unruly at first, and I felt like I was going down a dead end, but I found that there was a way through it, given certain 'helps'.

Significantly, there were echoes of my experience in that of Ignatius of Loyola. He was a vain and arrogant soldier who was forced by a battlefield injury into many months of recuperation. While daydreaming about romance and outdoing the saints, he noticed that the two opposing types of daydreams left him feeling different inside – one left him empty and dry, the other happy and content. The Ignatian system of spirituality is based on this foundational experience of noticing the internal effects of different 'spirits' or moods. This is often referred to as 'the Discernment of Spirits'.

The first step was to move away from the 'childlike' image of God and of faith I had inherited and rather step into the mess of my inner life! I want to share with you the fifteen things I discovered when I took this inward journey.

The Discernment of Spirits: the interpretation of what Ignatius Loyola called the 'motions of the soul'. These interior movements consist of thoughts, imaginings, emotions, inclinations, desires, feelings, repulsions, and attractions. Spiritual Discernment of Spirits involves becoming sensitive to these movements, reflecting on them, and understanding where they come from and where they lead us. See www.ignatianspirituality.com/making-good-decisions/discernment-of-spirits/ for more.

Point 1

God is found easier within and not without

It seems counter-intuitive to find God within yourself. It seems so subjective and almost 'New Age'. However, as St Augustine says, God is closer to you than you are to yourself. It seems too good to be true, that you have been created by God and that God holds you in being, cradled and loved. If you have been created by God, then there must be a way of 'keeping in touch' with God, of maintaining constant contact. It is a wondrous thing that God could be so close and interested in people that it should transform the way people pray and live. Often, however, people get discouraged and doubt themselves and God. They can't connect this 'inner fire' or passion with their notion of God. More often, it is the agnostic or atheistic voice that gets heard: God has abandoned me, doesn't care or doesn't exist at all. Yet, in my moments of clarity I recognise an inner voice, especially at key moments of crisis or change. You don't need to be afraid of moments of crisis or change, because God is present in those moments. They can even have very positive, unexpected effects! In my life, a moment of crisis over my career led to a very positive change. I joined the Jesuits.

GROWING YOUR IMAGE OF GOD

Rather than sitting in judgement of me from far above, God is actually in touch with me in a constant and loving way.

In times of crisis, I can find God within me.

Point 2

God is always trying
to communicate with you

There is a 'message' that is always being transmitted and you have to 'tune in' to that frequency. God is looking for a *relationship*, a two-way communication where there is interaction and movement. Prayer involves a lot of listening. Sometimes spoken prayers can be too much about me talking, asking for what I want, and therefore there is no listening. The static image of God is dominated by communication that only goes one way: either I continually ask God for things that I want or the opposite, God continually sends me commandments and instructions on what to do. Neither of these catch the dynamic nature of a relationship or the intimacy and warmth of it. A loving relationship transforms the way I want to be close with the 'beloved'. Ignatius talks of it as a conversation between close friends, alternating between talking and listening, always working towards the good.

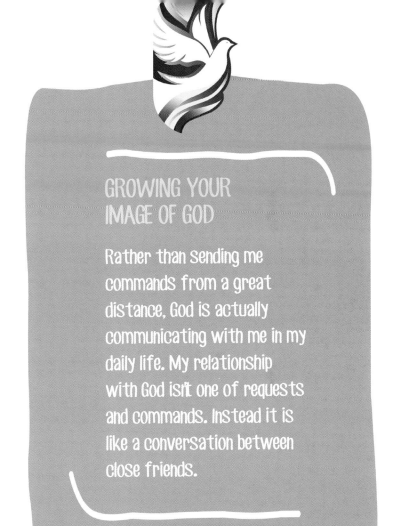

GROWING YOUR
IMAGE OF GOD

Rather than sending me commands from a great distance, God is actually communicating with me in my daily life. My relationship with God isn't one of requests and commands. Instead it is like a conversation between close friends.

Point 3

God can communicate
with you through anything

The Ignatian phrase used is: 'finding God in all things'. All the things of this world are part of God's creation and have the potential to bring you towards or away from God. It all depends on your attitude or attachment to these things. Something you value such as money, a car, a computer can be a tool to connect with others and make their lives better, or it can become part of your private horde that you keep for yourself. Self-knowledge and awareness is needed if you want to examine yourself and how you use the things of the world.

The key place to find God is within yourself. For example, in Ignatius's devastating battle injury, God was using his daydreams to draw him towards certain life-giving things and away from others. His personal chivalric 'heroism' and plans for glory were dashed and exposed. Instead, he realised that God was calling him to a radically different life of pilgrimage, selfless service and helping others. The injury, rather than being the disaster he thought it was, was actually the beginning of a new life with God at the centre.

GROWING YOUR IMAGE OF GOD

Just like in the life of Ignatius, God may be communicating with you in unexpected ways. God may even be communicating with you through something that seems initially bad or disastrous (like getting ill for example)! God doesn't need a burning bush: people, places, experiences, books, movies, even the internet can be points of contact with God.

Point 4

God is in your deepest desires, not in the superficial ones

On a retreat in 1990, while I was still in the computer business, I remember an old friar telling me that while most people initially live according to a set purpose or goal (success, money, fame, etc.), they later come to focus on doing something meaningful, something that helps others. This was exactly my experience. Working in business, I quickly got all the material possessions and status I thought I desired (superficial desire), but it was a desolate, empty experience and prompted a search for my true vocation as a priest (deeper desire). While not everyone is going to be a priest, it does highlight that each person has something unique to offer and happiness consists in working with this for others. There are often a lot of dead ends on this road of discovery, however. You cannot allow ego or selfish indulgence to extinguish your fragile, inner flame. Ignatian spirituality captures this tension perfectly: the soul is given enormous freedom and responsibility, faces the inevitable choices and dilemmas of life, and sees where it comes alive.

GROWING YOUR IMAGE OF GOD

You can see how different the 'childlike' and 'mature' images of God are! Sometimes God is presented as an authority figure commanding you to live a certain way. In an Ignatian context, you are invited to see God as giving you great freedom and responsibility to make difficult choices and to follow your inner flame.

Point 5

Stop and look back or reflect

God is in relationship with me, and I am able to experience that relationship directly. However, to tune in to this reality, I need time and space to reflect, to be able to see clearly what is going on. I have to be sensitive and tuned in to listen to the message. It is a skill that can be developed. There is something uniquely human about consciousness and this capacity for reflection or self-awareness. This consciousness gives human beings the ability to look at themselves, to stand outside themselves and evaluate their experience. Often modern culture has written off this aspect as 'navel gazing' or time wasting with its productive and consumerist emphasis. However, there has been a recovery of this aspect of humanity in recent years with the growth of meditation, self-awareness, holistic education and process-oriented psychology. Ignatian spirituality has shown itself particularly useful in speaking to a post-modern world because it focuses on subjective experience as a gateway to the spiritual dimension of life.

GROWING YOUR IMAGE OF GOD

In the past you might have waited to hear the voice of God in a miracle or a clap of thunder. Now that you know that God is always communicating with you, you can see that tuning in to God is a skill to be learned and improved on, rather than a gift given only to some.

19

Point 6

God works with you in the essence of your humanity

Because you are a human, organic, developmental being, you work in stages or steps in what is a process of growth. God leads you gently and progressively through these stages of growth and change. Generally, God does not work suddenly or miraculously, and very seldom outside the human condition. Even St Paul's 'conversion' took ten years. Genuine conversion is a gradual process that works in harmony with your humanity. The rush to dramatic or quick answers often doesn't lead to good solutions, rather what's important is a balanced approach that respects both the human process and the slow, patient work of God. This normally happens over time and space, just like other processes of growth in nature, rather than dramatic thunderbolts or instant conversions. In my case it was working with a Jesuit spiritual guide on what to do with my life in 1991. Over two years we built up trust, I learned how to pray, and we began to explore vocation options. The best solution was this real engagement, a relationship with this trusted guide, called a spiritual director, that allowed for a gradual exploration of options and priorities over time.

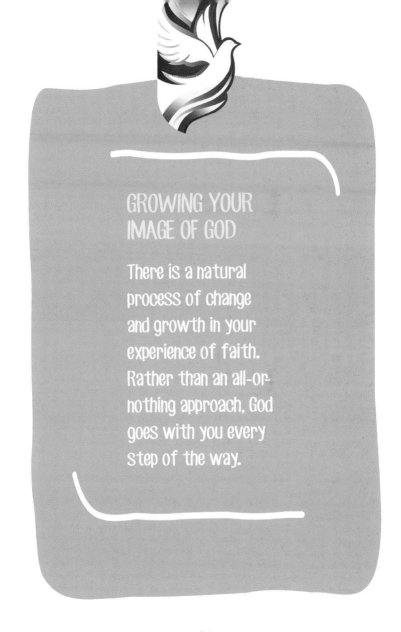

GROWING YOUR
IMAGE OF GOD

There is a natural process of change and growth in your experience of faith. Rather than an all-or-nothing approach, God goes with you every step of the way.

Point 7

Two different forces working on you

*T*he key insight of Ignatius is that there are two voices speaking to you at any moment: one is from God and is life-giving, while the other Ignatius calls the 'enemy of human nature' and is life-draining or life-sapping. While this is primarily a spiritual insight, it obviously has huge implications for mental health and psychological well-being. Ultimately, it boils down to consistently making life-enhancing decisions, tackling the seductive demons and unmasking them. Ignatius eventually developed a whole system for differentiating the voices called the Discernment of Spirits, to help people be wise to the enemy's deceptions and attempts at sabotage. Your challenge is to examine or sift your experience, like panning for gold to separate the dross from the gold nuggets. This is discernment: the process of working out where God is calling and taking action in line with that. This will involve prayer and reflection, and journalling and talking it over with a 'trusted other' can be helpful too.

GROWING YOUR IMAGE OF GOD

It's not always obvious or clear what God is calling you to do. A process of discernment is required. There is gold in your own experience, you just have to know how to find it!

Point 8

From conscience to consciousness

There is an old idea of conscience as a kind of moral 'superego' that guides with stings of remorse and guilt. This is helpful up to a point, but what is more helpful is the broader idea that God is guiding me in all aspects of my life and in the very stream of consciousness that I'm immersed in. I need to be aware of everyting that's going on inside and out, in order to be more responsive, active and creative in responding to the challenges of the world. This broader view sees morality in the bigger picture, beyond commandments and rules, in the essence of what it is to be human. God, my creator, wants me to be free, fully engaged with the world and finding happiness in it. Ultimately, it's about being at peace with myself and my life, that very illusive inner happiness that no amount of money, possessions, drink or drugs will bring. Inevitably this involves choosing 'the road less travelled', 'ploughing your own furrow', and stepping out of the comfort zone of expectations, roles and customs, to be authentic, true and real. It is an exciting journey, and you will feel alive as never before.

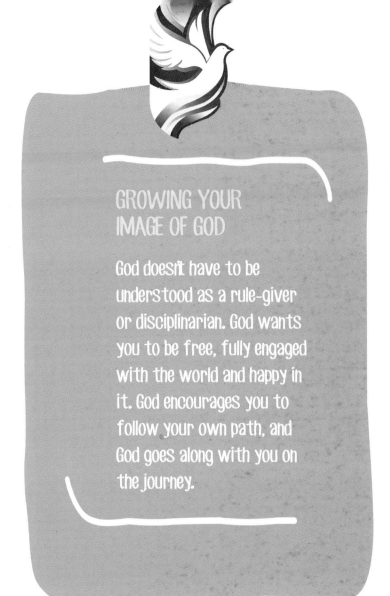

GROWING YOUR IMAGE OF GOD

God doesn't have to be understood as a rule-giver or disciplinarian. God wants you to be free, fully engaged with the world and happy in it. God encourages you to follow your own path, and God goes along with you on the journey.

It's about what you do

Ultimately, spirituality boils down to decisions and actions. The person of Jesus is enormously attractive as he is always real, compassionate and on the move. Therefore, the goal of life is to be like Christ in the world, to put on the mind of Christ (Philippians 2:5–8) and to live like Jesus did: conscious of his dependence on the Father and figuring out how to follow God's will in making God's love tangible and real. If you really believe in the humanity of Jesus and the consequences of the Incarnation (1 John 1:1–2), you are called to be an imitator, follower and disciple of God. You have to live your life in the same pilgrim way that Jesus did, depending on the Father for everything and not getting too attached to any of the things of the world. Inevitably, this brings you to your true calling or vocation, which almost always results in helping others or being of service to heal a broken world (God always brings you out of yourself and towards others).

GROWING YOUR IMAGE OF GOD

There are many ways to
understand spirituality.
One way is to focus on
decisions and actions.
You are encouraged by
God to take action, to
go out into the world
and to participate in
healing it.

Point 10

Freedom

The word freedom is frequently misunderstood in today's culture. It is typically interpreted as 'freedom from' restrictions or limitations on individual choices (e.g. lying on a beach without a care in the world). However, often this can simply be a disguised selfishness with associated negative consequences as wealth, possessions and lack of commitments are prioritised. This results in an impoverished experience of 'freedom' that isn't true freedom. The Ignatian concept of freedom as 'freedom for' is much more useful. This is a sense of service and responsibility to others that helps people to sacrifice individual freedom for a greater end: the care of others, the construction of an inclusive society and reaching out to the vulnerable.

At the heart of this, however, is acknowledging that often you are not free. You have many distractions, dependencies and even addictions that keep you in chains and away from God and indeed, from life. Ignatius knew this reality too, all the vanity and egoism that is so much a part of being human and which needs to be worked on. The Ignatian approach is to name the things that hold you back and to ask for God's help in overcoming them. Making a prayer of it helps you to be more free, to loosen the shackles a little bit every time and come closer to God.

GROWING YOUR IMAGE OF GOD

The freedom God wants for you is different from freedom as it is understood in todays culture. It is a 'freedom for' rather than a 'freedom from'. God invites you to be free to work toward a greater end: the care of others and the building of an inclusive society.

Point 11

The U-shaped Curve

The life and death of Jesus is not something that happened years ago and which is no longer relevant. Rather it is the very essence of your life. The U-shaped curve of dying and rising is a continual process that marks your life and shapes your world. How do I know this? From life's experience of the process of suffering and pain that alternates with great joy and fulfilment. Like a pilgrim journey, there are always hills and valleys, peaks and troughs, high points and low points. It is never controllable or predictable however, and we have to adapt to what life throws at us. This is where real prayer comes in, the prayer of the cross, abandoning control and letting God take over. Jesus is the one who has been there before you in the depths, and who has taken the hit for you. It helps me to live through these inevitable moments of darkness. Praying through pain, I begin to pull out of the dive. I begin to rise again. I can see a way. I walk towards the light. I am walking in faith, hope and love abound.

GROWING YOUR
IMAGE OF GOD

The life and death of Jesus is not something that happened in the distant past. It's something that is right at the heart of your life. The U-shaped curve of dying and rising is something evident in your own experience of life.

Point 12

Using the head and heart

Is Ignatian spirituality too focused on the inner life of people? Does focus on people's feelings and moods lead to the neglect of the more rational and institutional aspects of faith? Some people think so. Michael J O'Sullivan SJ once wrote that people should 'trust their feelings, but use their head'. This was how he described discernment in the Ignatian tradition. I think this captures the essence of a 'both and' approach. In any solid spirituality the heart and head have to be in dialogue! Ignatian spirituality does not call for you to focus only on your feelings and moods, even though these do play an important part in your spiritual journey. Rather, Ignatian spirituality encourages you to look at *both* heart and head when making a decision. Sometimes you may feel strongly that a certain decision is the right one, but talking it through rationally and dispassionately may help you to see it in a different light. Equally, it might be that a decision makes perfect sense on paper, but your heart is not in it. Both the head and the heart have a role to play in discernment and decision-making!

GROWING YOUR
IMAGE OF GOD

God is always communicating
with you, and God wants
you to be free to affect
the world in a positive way.
Your head and your heart
both have a role to play in
this. You shouldn't neglect the
rational or emotive aspects
of faith.

Point 13

Going inwards to work outwards

Often when people think of meditation and prayer, they think of it as an escape from the world and responsibilities. For Ignatius the inner journey of confronting his demons and finding God led eventually to a great compassion for the poor and the suffering. There is a value in becoming aware and conscious of your 'inner world' of feelings and desires. It helps you to navigate the complexity of the objective 'outer world'. Your actions have sigificance; it is important what you do, and there *is* meaning and truth to be found. All is not relative or subjective. God normally is inviting us to take some concrete step of action to help others. The world needs you to be a responsible, active agent for change and justice.

GROWING YOUR IMAGE OF GOD

A rich inner life of faith does not have to be closed off from the outside world. God knows that your inner life and the outer world are connected. Understanding your inner life can help you to better act in an often overwhelming and confusing outer world.

Point 14

As an individual you need community

Very quickly after his conversion, Ignatius Loyola set about building a group of like-minded individuals. Not only were they setting up a new kind of religious community (mission focused), but they were in dialogue with the church and tradition. Left to their own devices, it is all too easy for people to get off track, to get caught up in the ego (selfishness), and to rationalise and justify all sorts of things.

People need support in terms of other spiritual guides and a supportive Christian community to help them stay focused. Being part of a tradition means that there are checks and balances. There is a sense of accumulated wisdom and learning from the past, especially when it comes to what have proven to be dead ends.

GROWING YOUR IMAGE OF GOD

The Christian community and
its accumulated wisdom is
part of God's gift to you.
At times the traditions of
the Church may have felt like
they weighed you down or
were inaccessible to you. God
offers them as a support
system.

Point 15

Reliving the experience of the Gospels

The Gospel texts recount the radical change brought about in the disciples in encountering the risen Christ. Jesus is the ultimate example of living an aware, reflective life, and being connected to God and self. His whole existence is a being there for others and being radically free to love. The passion and death of Jesus is the story of the greatest love that anyone can give. Accordingly, Christians live from the resurrection, the Spirit dwelling within us. This is the Spirit of love, of forgiveness, that wants to bring us back to our true selves; there is nothing that can separate us from the love of God (Romans 8:39) and God is love (1 John 4:8). This God is a living reality, not an idea or concept, that transforms our hearts and makes life meaningful.

GROWING YOUR
IMAGE OF GOD

God is not remote from you. God is not in the past, nor is God 'in the clouds'. God is a living reality, and the Spirit of God lives within you.

Tips for Building a Spiritual Life

Like any other part of life, the spiritual life has to be worked at, supported, planned for, prioritised and studied. There are a number of obvious things that are part of it.

Prayer or meditation in its many forms is central as the 'input' to the system; this is being able to receive love from God in order to give it. The most useful Ignatian prayer of reflection is the daily Examen, a chance to review the day and see where God has been: https://www.ignatianspirituality. com/ignatian-prayer/the-examen.

Having a spiritual guide or director is useful to help you get perspective, make sure that you are not caught up in your own ego, and that you are really following what God wants and what is genuinely good for you: someone else can see more easily than you can what is going on in your inner life. Normally this is someone with qualifications and training.

Spiritual reading is helpful to understand that others have walked this path before you, that there is a body of wisdom and experience that give you indications of what works and what doesn't; the Bible is the privileged example of how people have looked for God in different times and cultures (the Old Testament) and in Jesus we can see God working directly (the New Testament). Taking an introductory course in theology or spirituality is also helpful to move forward in the spiritual life.

Being part of a community of fellow searchers and seekers is essential to get support and keep the focus, especially when times get tough. Some churches have prayer groups, bible study or life-experience 'sharing' groups that support the spiritual life, offer a space to search and ask questions, and make it easier than being alone. Ritual, sacrament and Eucharist are the public, communal part of personal spiritual life, where people come together to celebrate faith; the symbols and rituals come alive as they are rooted in your experience and that of the community.

Having regular opportunities to go on retreat, to step out of the normal rhythm of life and business, are key to nurturing the spiritual life. It is only in silence and reflection that you can do the necessary listening to get perspective and direction. Many parishes and religious centres offer programmes in specialised 'retreat houses or centres' that provide a spiritual director, silence and a programme of meditations that greatly helps the process. Normally people go for a weekend or week-long retreat, although other options are also available whereby you can do a retreat integrated with your daily life.

It is all about what you do; decisions and actions speak louder than words. Christianity is about doing what Christ did – being there for others, not judging others and above all, acting with compassion. It can mean choosing jobs and careers that are about more than money. It has to be from the heart and it has to mean something, to make a difference in the world.

Obviously, you need to look after yourself, to look after the practicalities of your health, body, diet, and of your job, career, or vocation. You need rest and relaxation, time for family, etc. These are basic minimums that can affect your spiritual life negatively if they are not right.

Conclusion

Spirituality is about 'channelling the inner fire', choosing life over death, awareness over unconsciousness, becoming fully alive and human, just like Jesus was. You are similarly called to live like Christ, to let go of fear (the opposite of love) and to trust in God's plan. Understanding the humanity of Christ, which we all share, is key to understanding your own humanity and how you should live.

God is at work in your life right now. Your job is to uncover the subtle messages that God is communicating to you, to be in dynamic relationship with God and to be at peace with the world and yourself. It is a lot more about 'letting go' and abandoning yourself to the reality of what *is*, rather that trying to make things happen through your efforts. This is a personal journey that everyone has to make for themselves, though having companions and support is crucial to making it possible. This does not promise an easy or a comfortable life; it is a call to follow Christ himself, to let go of the things of this world and to be engaged in the wider mission for which you were born to become an active agent or collaborator for God's love in the world. Good luck with it!

Helpful Links and Further Reading

Helpful links

The life of Ignatius:
www.jesuits.org/stories/the-life-of-st-ignatius-of-loyola/

SEEL (The Spiritual Exercises in Daily Life) is a Jesuit-organised programme of meditations that can be done at home, see:
www.manresa.ie/ignatian-spirituality/exercises-in-daily-life

Jesuit Centre of Spirituality, Manresa, Dublin:
www.manresa.ie/

Retreat centres in Ireland: www.catholicireland.net/retreats/

Retreat centres in the UK: www.retreats.org.uk/findaretreat

Further reading

Gerard Hughes, *God of Surprises*
Anthony de Mello, *Awareness*
Anthony de Mello, *Sadhana: A Way to God*
Brian Grogan, *Finding God in All Things*
Jim Maher, *Pathways to a Decision with Ignatius Loyola*
Brendan McManus, *The Way to Manresa*
Brendan McManus & Jim Deeds, *Finding God in the Mess*
Morgan Scott Peck, *The Road Less Travelled*

Finding God
in the Mess

Meditations for Mindful Living

Jim Deeds & Brendan McManus SJ

www.messenger.ie

DEEPER into the MESS
the MESS
Praying Through Tough Times

Brendan McManus SJ and Jim Deeds

www.messenger.ie

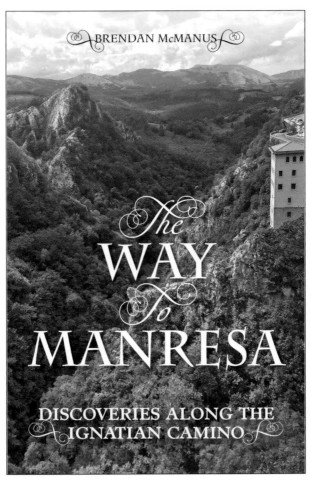

BRENDAN McMANUS

The
WAY
To
MANRESA

DISCOVERIES ALONG THE
IGNATIAN CAMINO

www.messenger.ie

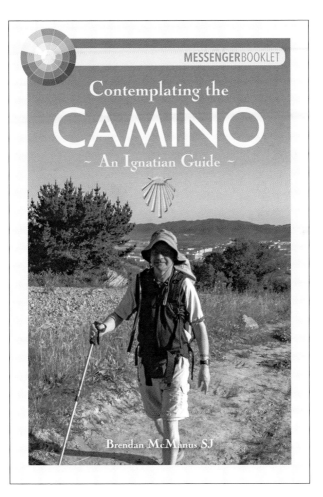

www.messenger.ie